# Problem Solving & Reasoning Activity Book

## for ages 7-8

This CGP book is bursting with fun activities to build up children's skills and confidence.

It's ideal for extra practice to reinforce what they're learning in primary school. Enjoy!

Published by CGP

Editors:
Michael Bushell, Liam Dyer, Sean McParland and Alison Palin

Proofreaders:
Gail Renaud and Glenn Rogers

With thanks to Emily Smith for the copyright research.

ISBN: 978 1 78908 709 3

Image of 10 pence coin used on page 17 © iStock.com/john shepherd, 20 pence coin used on page 17 © iStock.com/Jaap2, 50 pence coin and £2 coin used on page 17 © iStock.com/duncan1890, £1 coin used on page 17 © iStock.com/ LPETTET

Graphics used on the cover and throughout the book © www.edu-clips.com
Cover design concept by emc design ltd.

Printed by W&G Baird Ltd, Antrim.

Text, design, layout and original illustrations © Coordination Group Publications Ltd. (CGP) 2020
All rights reserved.

Photocopying this book is not permitted, even if you have a CLA licence.
Extra copies are available from CGP with next day delivery • 0800 1712 712 • www.cgpbooks.co.uk

# Contents

| | |
|---|---|
| Working with Numbers 1 | 2 |
| Working with Numbers 2 | 4 |
| Adding and Subtracting | 6 |
| Multiplying and Dividing | 8 |
| Fractions | 10 |
| Measuring | 12 |
| | |
| Puzzle: Mascot Muddle | 14 |
| | |
| Money | 16 |
| Time | 18 |
| Shapes | 20 |
| Angles and Lines | 22 |
| Charts and Tables | 24 |
| Mixed Problems | 26 |
| | |
| Answers | 28 |

# Working with Numbers 1

## How It Works

You need to know the values of the digits in a number.

This is **three hundred and sixteen**.

The **3** digit shows **3** hundreds.
The **1** digit shows **1** ten.
The **6** digit shows **6** ones.

You can **partition** (break up) a number into a sum of other numbers. For example, you can partition 316 into 300 + 10 + 6.

## Now Try These

1. Draw lines to match each tub of popcorn to the correct number in words.

768
186
511
932

One hundred...    ...and eleven
Nine hundred...    ...and eighty-six
Five hundred...    ...and sixty-eight
Seven hundred...    ...and thirty-two

2. Use each of the digits shown on these tickets to make:

2   6   3

a) The biggest 3-digit number possible.

..................

b) A 3-digit number with the ones digit twice as big as the hundreds digit.

..................

3. These film posters show how many people saw each film on its first day.

 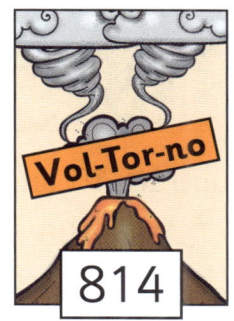  

Super-Keith: 726   Vol-Tor-no: 814   Deer Deer: 786

The number who saw Jigsaw Attack has the same hundreds digit as Super-Keith, the same tens digit as Deer Deer and the same ones digit as Vol-Tor-no.

Circle the posters of the films that more people saw than Jigsaw Attack.

4. Beth, Matt and Asha talk about the number of minutes they spent at the cinema one month. How many minutes did Asha spend at the cinema?

Beth: My number is made by adding 4 hundreds, 3 tens and 7 ones.

Matt: My number has 2 more hundreds and 5 fewer ones than Beth's number.

Asha: My number has 3 fewer hundreds and 6 more tens than Matt's number.

.................... minutes

## An Extra Challenge

Rhys uses large, medium and small drinks to show some 3-digit numbers.

→ 231

a) What number do these drinks show?

b) Rhys swaps each small drink from part a) for a large one.

What number is shown now?

How did you do? Would you give your work a 5-star review?

# Working with Numbers 2

## How It Works

You can use your place value skills to add or subtract 10 and 100.

To find **10** more or less, add or subtract 1 from the **tens** digit.

10 less    10 more
**238** ← **248** → **258**
4 − 1 = 3    4 + 1 = 5

To find **100** more or less, add or subtract 1 from the **hundreds** digit.

100 less    100 more
**148** ← **248** → **348**
2 − 1 = 1    2 + 1 = 3

## Now Try These

1. Some of the numbers in these patterns are hidden by footprints.

   0    50    100    ✋    200    250    ✋    ✋

   0    ✋    200    ✋    ✋    500    600    700

   What number is hidden in **both** patterns?

   ...........................

2. Estimate the numbers that these arrows are pointing to.

   a)  300    260    220    180    140    100
       ←——+——+——+——+——+——+——→
                    ↑
                 [    ]

   b)  350    425    475  495    560    600
       ←——+——+——+——+——+——+——→
                   ↑
                 [    ]

4

3. Two beavers start counting from zero and say some of the numbers on these logs. Brooke counts in steps of 4 and Nora counts in steps of 8.

Circle the correct name and write the missing number to finish this sentence.

Brooke / Nora says ............... more of the numbers.

4. Tammy's dam is made up of 627 sticks.
100 sticks are washed away in a storm, so she adds the sticks below.

How many sticks are in the dam now?

........................... sticks

## An Extra Challenge

Use Frank's clues to work out how many twigs are in his bundle.

I found the number this arrow is pointing to.

I took the **digit** in the tens place...

...and added 3...

...then counted up 5 times in steps of 4.

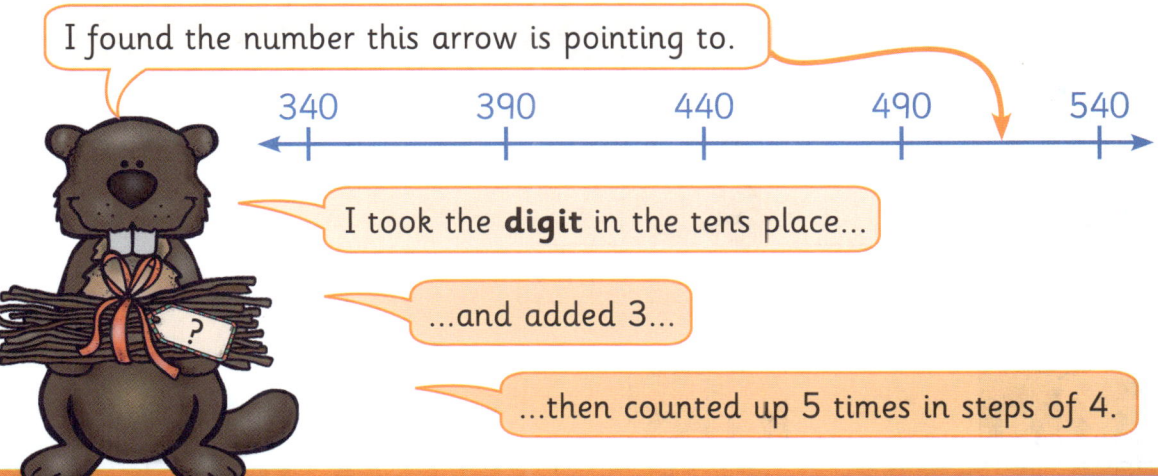

Are you eager to solve some more problems on numbers?

# Adding and Subtracting

## How It Works

You might need to use **inverse calculations** in addition and subtraction problems. Have a look at this example:

Find the missing number in the sum 324 + ? = 524.

The inverse of addition is subtraction, so subtract 324 to find the missing number.

? = 524 − 324 = 200, so the missing number is **200**.

## Now Try These

1. Parts of these calculations are hidden behind things headed for the compost bin. What number is each thing hiding?

   120 +  = 210     → ........................

    + 475 = 675     → ........................

    − 340 = 530     → ........................

2. The numbers of bottles and boxes collected at a recycling centre are shown below. How many more bottles than boxes did the centre collect over the two days?

   Monday: 318 bottles    Tuesday: 241 bottles

   Monday and Tuesday: 472 boxes in total

   ........................ bottles

3. Use the sum in the box to help you answer these problems.  $60 + 25 = 85$

   a) Circle the bottle that shows the answer to $600 + 250$.

   b) Colour in the bin that does **not** hold the answer to either $400 + 250$ or $600 + 150$.

4. Fill in the missing digits in each of these calculations.

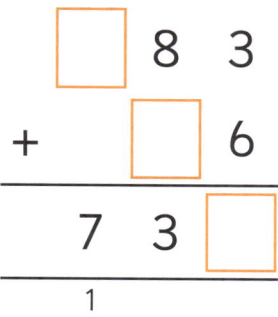
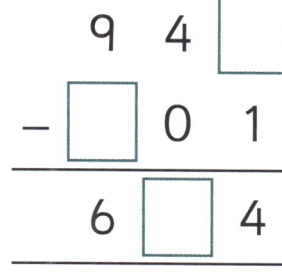
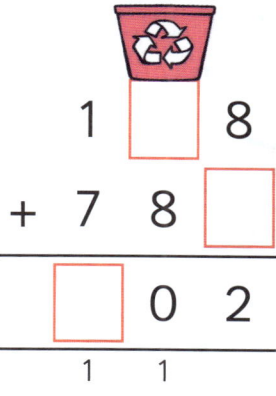

## An Extra Challenge

Daksh is sorting his recycling into three bins.
Only items whose calculations have certain answers are allowed in each bin.

Which items are allowed in more than one of the bins?

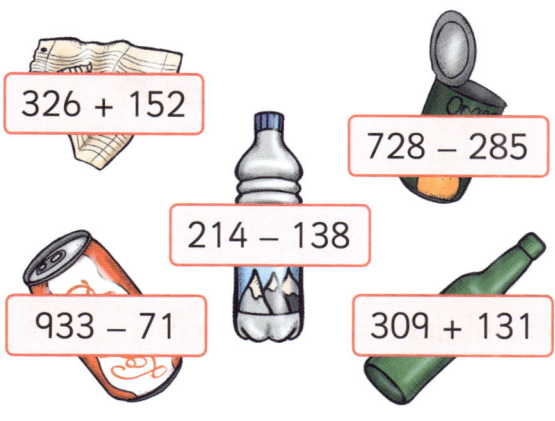

Has working with addition and subtraction bin good for you?

# Multiplying and Dividing

## How It Works

You can use times tables to solve all sorts of problems — here's an example:

A swimming club buys caps in packs of **32**.
How many caps are there in **4** packs?

Partition the big number. → 32 = 30 + 2
Multiply each part. → 30 × 4 = 120, 2 × 4 = 8
Add the results together. → 120 + 8 = **128 caps**

30 is 10 times bigger than 3, so 30 × 4 is 10 times bigger than 3 × 4.

## Now Try These

1. Fill in the boxes to complete the calculations.

4 × 10 × ☐ = 80

2 × ☐ × 3 = 60

2. Work out the answer to each calculation. Dan's favourite T-shirt has the answer closest to the answer for his shorts. Tick (✔) the box below his favourite T-shirt.

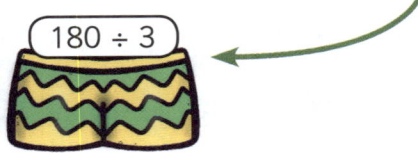
180 ÷ 3

33 × 2

13 × 5

4 × 16

3. A pool is split into three lanes. Each lane has the same number of swimmers. Circle the **two** numbers that **cannot** be the total number of swimmers.

15    16    17    18

4. Kaila takes 43 strokes to swim the length of a pool.
   How many strokes does she take to swim 8 lengths?

.................... strokes

5. Jayden has made this recipe for pink lemonade.

   **Pink Lemonade (2 cups)**
   3 lemons
   2 oranges
   160 g raspberries
   400 ml of water

   a) How many lemons are needed to make 4 cups?

   ................ lemons

   b) How much water is needed to make:

   (i) 1 cup?                (ii) 3 cups?

   .................... ml          .................... ml

6. Tami sees 4 swimming costumes and 3 inflatable toys in a shop.

   How many different ways could Tami pick one costume and one toy?

   ................ ways

## An Extra Challenge

Amaya is making lemonade using Jayden's recipe shown above.
She can buy lemons in packs of four and oranges in packs of three.

She buys 6 packs of lemons and 6 packs of oranges.

How many cups of lemonade could she make with these ingredients?
(She has enough raspberries and water.)

Did that all go swimmingly?
Tick a box to show how you feel.

# Fractions

## How It Works

You can find **fractions** of a set of objects or an amount:
$\frac{2}{6}$ of these crystals are green and $\frac{1}{6}$ are orange.

You can also **add** or **subtract** fractions:

The green and orange crystals make up $\frac{2}{6} + \frac{1}{6} = \frac{3}{6}$.

The other $\frac{6}{6} - \frac{3}{6} = \frac{3}{6}$ of the crystals are purple.

## Now Try These

1. Eli, Josh and Kate are looking for gold.

    a) $\frac{2}{3}$ of Eli's nuggets are gold.

    Colour more nuggets below to show $\frac{2}{3}$ of the nuggets.

    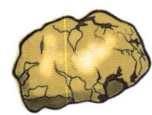     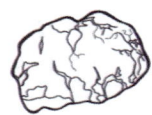

    b) Write their names in order of the fraction of nuggets they each have that are gold, going from largest to smallest.

    .................... largest

    ....................

    .................... smallest

2. Doug finds these pieces of amber.

    a) What fraction of the pieces of amber have a beetle inside?

    ....................

    b) Doug finds 20 more pieces of amber. The same fraction of these have a beetle inside. How many more beetles is this?

    .................... beetles

3. Fill in the boxes to make correct calculations.

$\frac{4}{7} + \frac{\square}{7} = \frac{6}{7}$   $\frac{\square}{8} - \frac{3}{8} = \frac{5}{8}$

$\frac{\square}{\square} + \frac{1}{6} = \frac{4}{6}$   $\frac{\square}{10} - \frac{2}{\square} = \frac{7}{10}$

Use this number line to help you with Question 4.

4. Haamid needs $\frac{4}{10}$ kg of coal to burn his fire for 15 minutes. How much coal does he need to burn his fire for:

   a) half an hour?    b) one hour?

   $\frac{\square}{\square}$ kg    $\square\frac{\square}{\square}$ kg

## An Extra Challenge

Sasha has written down the fraction of each type of rock and mineral she has in her collection:

quartz — $\frac{5}{10}$

sandstone — $\frac{2}{10}$

emerald — $\frac{3}{10}$

She has 6 pieces of emerald in her collection.

a) How many rocks and minerals does she have in total?
b) How many pieces of each of the other types does she have?

How were these pages?
Do fractions rock your world?

# Measuring

### How It Works

You need to be able to measure lengths, masses and volumes. Here's an example:

This scale is measuring mass in **grams** (g).

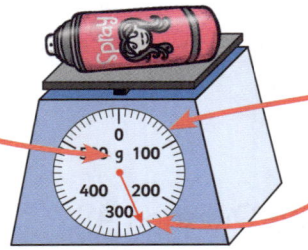

There are 10 small gaps between each hundred. Each measures 100 ÷ 10 = **10 g**.

So this hairspray has a mass of **260 g**.

### Now Try These

1. Fill in the boxes to show the length that each child is pointing to.

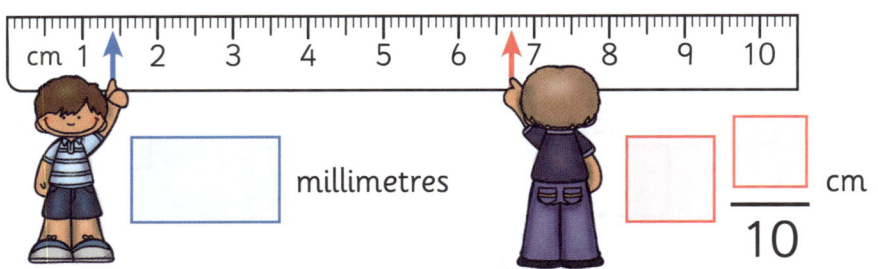

☐ millimetres      ☐ ☐ /10 cm

2. Jay's fringe was 80 mm long. He had 45 mm cut off and then 5 mm grew back. Colour in the picture on the right to show the length of his fringe now.

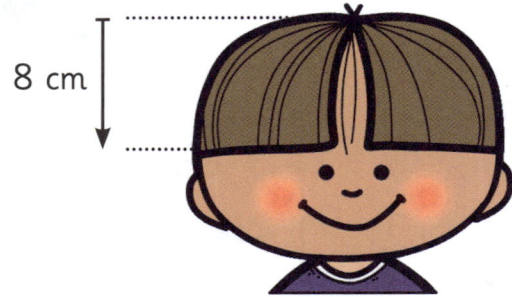

8 cm         2 cm

3. The two jugs show how much water is used to wash Lorna's hair.

   How many millilitres of water is this in total?

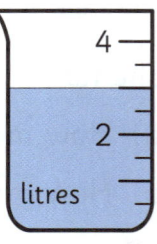

.................... ml

4. Draw lines to match each object to its most likely mass.

wall mirror    comb    hair dryer    moustache

15 kg    1500 g    $\frac{1}{4}$ g    20 g

5. a) The scales on the right show the mass of two hairbrushes. What is the mass of one hairbrush?

.................. g

b) The scales on the left show the mass of one hairbrush and a pair of scissors. What is the mass of the scissors?

.................. g

### An Extra Challenge

Zoey makes old-timey wigs. They should each have a plait that's longer than 20 cm and shorter than 23 cm. How many of these wigs have a plait with a correct length?

Were these problems head-scratchers for you?

# Mascot Muddle

People are voting for one of these five choices to be their sports club's new mascot.

Fred Fox | Sadie Storm | Wes Wolf | Seb Sun | Tia Tiger

Work out who everyone voted for. Tally up the votes as you go along to see which mascot won.

I voted for the mascot whose calculation has an answer with a 6 in the tens place.

My vote went to the mascot whose calculation has an answer equal to the missing number in 340 + ? = 530.

162 + 10     483 + 179

814 − 100    274 + 60    595 − 405

I have 7 books and 4 films. I voted for the mascot with the number of different ways I could pick one of each.

11     48

60     28     24

The mascot with the number missing in $\frac{1}{4}$ of ? = 12.

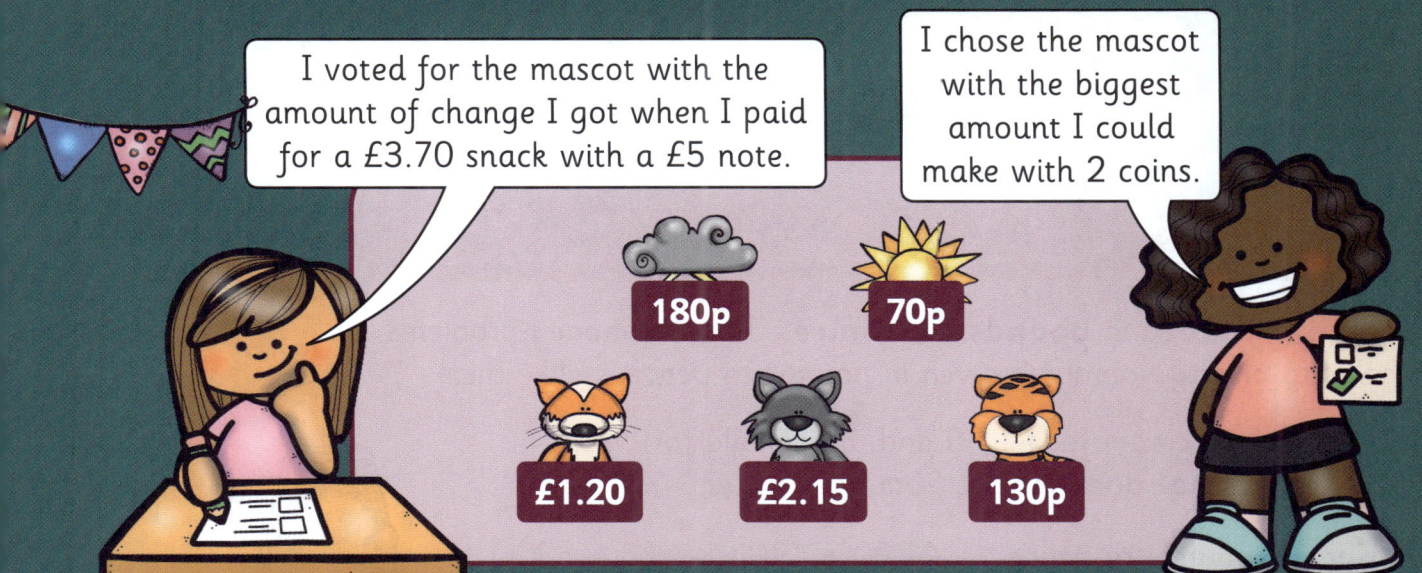

# Money

## How It Works

Money is measured in **pounds** and **pence**. To solve money problems, it helps to **change** amounts given in pounds to pence — like this:

Britta buys sun cream for £1.90 and an ice lolly for 80p. How much change does she get from a £5 note?

   Change pounds to pence:    £1.90 = 190p    £5 = 500p

   She pays 190p + 80p = 270p

   So she gets 500p − 270p = **230p** or **£2.30** as change.

## Now Try These

1. Put a tick (✔) below each window with a total less than £2.

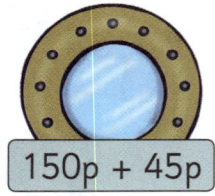

150p + 45p     £3 − 50p     £1.50 + 60p     £10 − £9.50

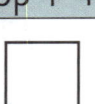

2. Rachel wants to go on a cruise that costs £300.
   She has saved £90 so far.
   How much more does she need to save?

   £.................

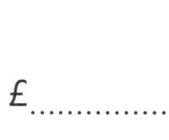
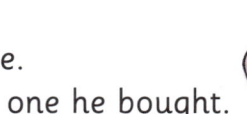

3. Eric pays £50 for a deckchair and gets £15 in change.
   Circle each deckchair below that costs more than the one he bought.

£35.50     £65.50     £33.50     £15.00

4. Lydia buys a pair of sunglasses. She pays exactly using 3 coins. Circle the amount that could be the cost of the sunglasses.

£4.15          £1.80          £2.60          £1.45

5. Look at the menu below.

**Shipshape Cafe**

| | |
|---|---|
| Pelican Punch | £2.85 |
| Seaweed Sandwich | £1.75 |
| Overboard Omelette | £3.90 |
| Sunshine Soup | 95p |

a) How much cheaper is a Sunshine Soup than an Overboard Omelette?

£ 

b) How much change will you get if you buy a Pelican Punch and a Seaweed Sandwich with £5?

£ 

### An Extra Challenge

Nylah left her purse on a ship! Her purse contains the change she was given when she paid with a £10 note for a dolphin keyring costing £4.80.

Three purses are in lost property. Which purse belongs to Nylah?

Oh buoy, that was lots of work! Did you cruise through it?

# Time

## How It Works

You need to know **seconds**, **minutes** and **hours**. Problems can get you to find **how long an event takes** or when it **starts** or **finishes**, like this example:

Ruben finished a tour around London at 4:30 pm.
He was on the tour for 2 hours 30 minutes. What time did it start?
Give your answer using the 24-hour clock.

4:30 pm —– 2 hours —→ 2:30 pm —– 30 minutes —→ 2:00 pm

2:00 pm is **14:00** in the 24-hour clock.

## Now Try These

1. Write the correct number on each telephone.

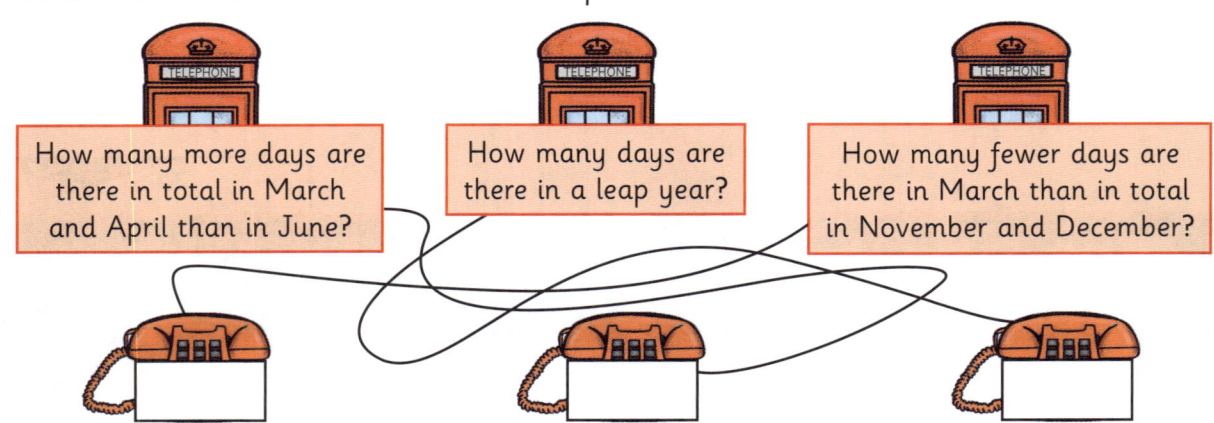

How many more days are there in total in March and April than in June?

How many days are there in a leap year?

How many fewer days are there in March than in total in November and December?

2. Two friends race across Tower Bridge.
Iain takes 2 minutes 10 seconds. Faruq takes 145 seconds.
What is the difference between their times?

.................... seconds

3. Amy visits a tea shop at ten past three in the afternoon.
She leaves two and a half hours later.

What time does she leave? Give your answer using the 12-hour clock.

............. : ....................

4. Here are the times of some bus journeys from Hyde Park.

| Destination | Leaves | Arrives |
|---|---|---|
| Heathrow | 09:45 | 10:35 |
| Liverpool Street | 10:15 | 10:55 |
| Canary Wharf | 10:55 | 11:50 |

a) How long is the journey to Canary Wharf?

.................... minutes

b) How much quicker is it to travel to Liverpool Street than Heathrow?

.................... minutes

5. Ethan looks at the clock tower on the right when he starts walking.
He is meeting a friend at 14:30.
It will take 30 minutes to walk there.
Estimate how many minutes early he will be.

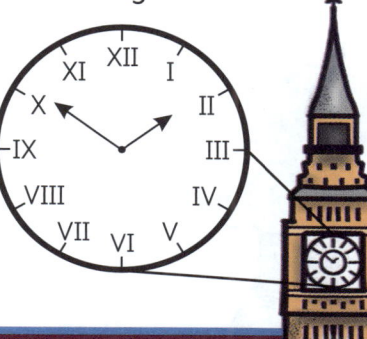

.................... minutes

## An Extra Challenge

The guard at a palace is replaced every **2 hours**.
Tim has been on guard there for **70 minutes**. It is now 12:15 pm.

a) When did Tim replace the last guard?

b) When will the next guard replace Tim?

Draw hands on these clocks to show your answers:

a)  am     b) 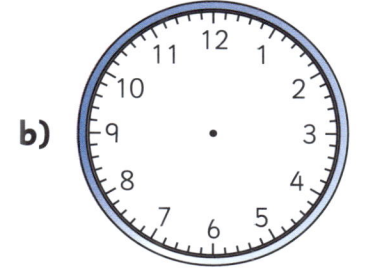 pm

How did that go? Tick a box... and please mind the gap.

# Shapes

## How It Works

These pages will test you on both **2D** and **3D** shape problems. Here's an example:

Look at the shapes on the right.
How many **triangular** faces are there?

There are **2** + **4** = **6 triangular faces**.

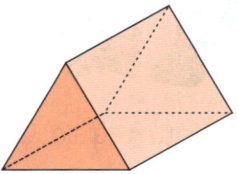 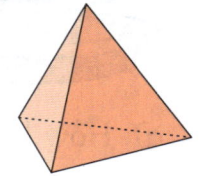

A triangular prism has **two** end faces that are triangles.

A triangle-based pyramid has **four** triangular faces.

## Now Try These

1. Complete the shapes on the grids to match the descriptions below.

My shape is regular. It has one more side than a triangle.

My shape is irregular. It has one less side than a hexagon.

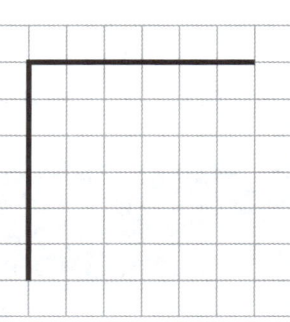

2. Look at the 3D shapes below.
Use words from the box to complete the sentences.

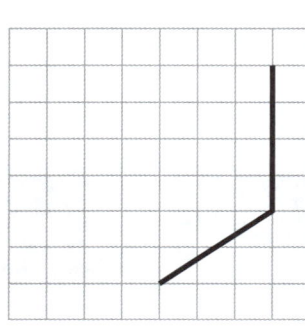

faces   five   vertices
pyramid   eight   cuboid
cylinder   circular

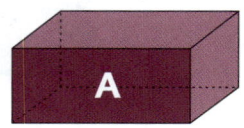 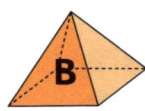 

a) Shape A has six ............................... .

b) Shape C is called a ............................... .

c) Shape B has ............................... edges.

d) Shape B has three fewer ............................... than Shape A.

3. Put a tick (✔) in the shape that has the shortest perimeter.

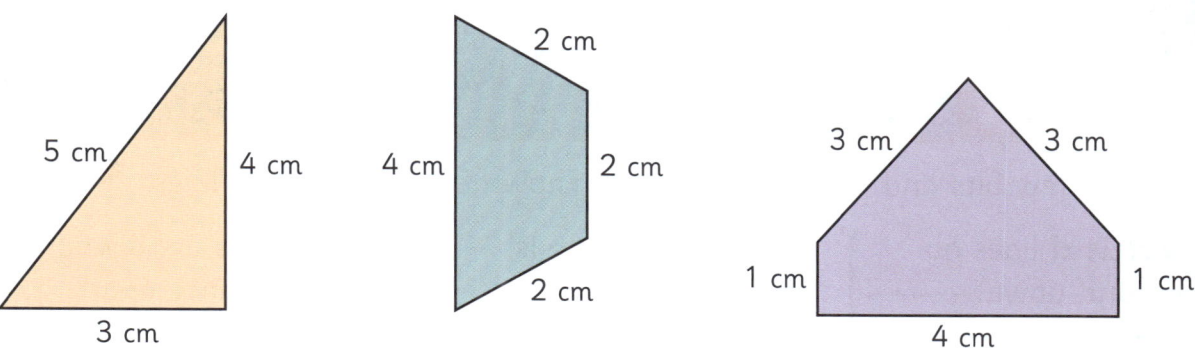

4. The shapes below are made out of these cubes. How many cubes do you need to build each shape?

   a)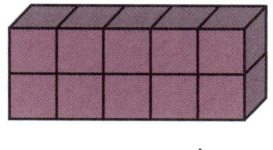

   .............. cubes

   b)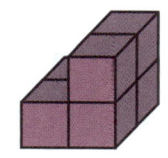

   .............. cubes

5. Betsy is thinking of a prism. The end faces are pentagons. How many vertices, edges and faces does her shape have?

   .................... vertices, .................... edges, .................... faces

## An Extra Challenge

Sean wants to design a new skate park. The sides of each square on this grid show 1 metre in real life.

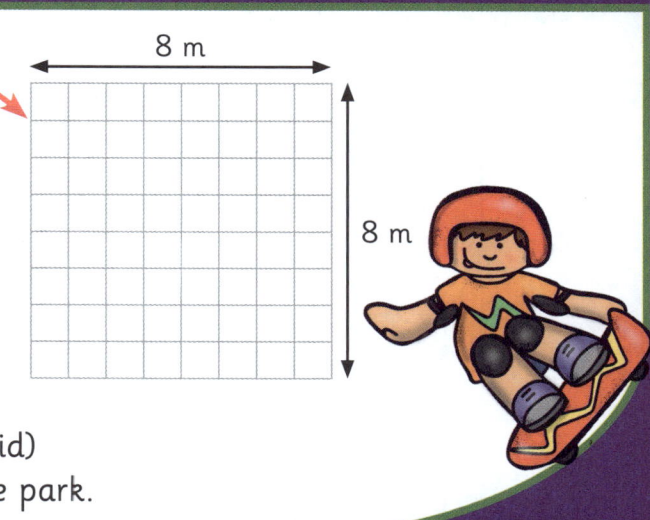

The park needs three **rectangular** zones:

- a **rail zone** with a perimeter of **18 m**.
- a **ramp zone** with a perimeter of **12 m**.
- a **rest zone** with a perimeter of **5 m**.

Use centimetre squared paper (or copy the grid) and draw **three** different designs for his skate park.

Good job on those problems! Now scoot over and tick a box!

21

# Angles and Lines

## How It Works

Here are a few bits and pieces you need to know about angles and lines.

**Vertical** lines go up and down.

**Horizontal** lines go from side to side.

A **right angle** is a quarter turn. It can be shown by a square.

**Parallel lines** are always the same distance apart.

**Perpendicular lines** meet at right angles.

A **clockwise** turn is in the same direction as the hands on a clock.

An **anticlockwise** turn is in the opposite direction.

## Now Try These

1. Lana is facing David's house.

   a) How many right angles clockwise must she turn to face Maria's house?

   ..................

   b) How many right angles anticlockwise must she turn to face Juan's house?

   ..................

2. In each part, colour in the shapes that are being described.

   a) This shape has more vertical sides than horizontal sides.

   b) These shapes have exactly three pairs of parallel sides.

3. Monty has made angles using spears.
   Circle the angles that are bigger than a right angle.

   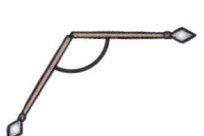  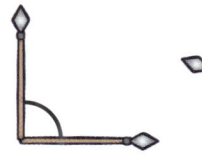 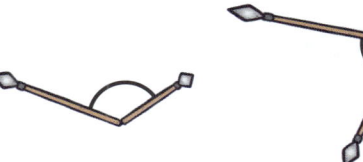

4. Kendra has painted shapes on these pots.
   How many vertices in each shape
   are made by perpendicular sides?

   A   B   C

   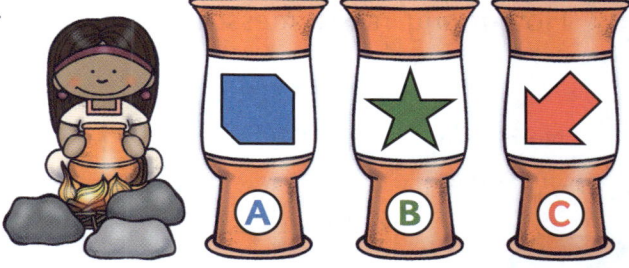

5. Each person turns their shield by the amount shown.
   Draw what each shield looks like after the turn.

   a) 3 right angles clockwise

   b) 5 right angles anticlockwise

## An Extra Challenge

a) Draw **two pairs** of **parallel lines** on each diagram.
   Every line must go through two dots and every dot must be used once.
   One has been done for you.

   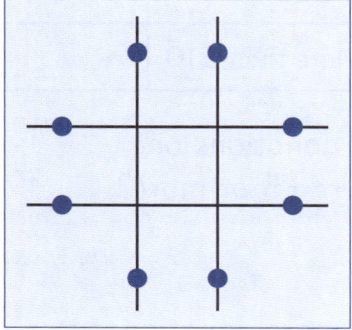 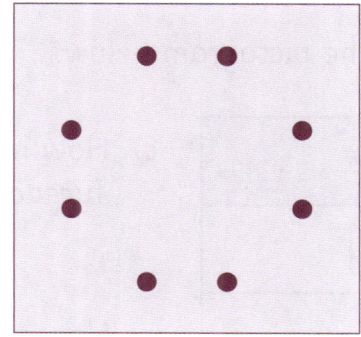

b) How many more ways can you find?

Are you a-maize-ing with angles and lines?

# Charts and Tables

## How It Works

You can solve problems by reading information from charts and tables — like this:

Mubin draws a **bar chart** to show how many messages he gets on his phone. How many **more** messages did he get on **Saturday** than on **Friday**?

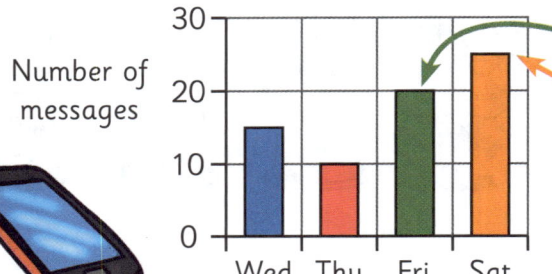

He got 20 messages on Friday.

This bar is halfway between 20 and 30, so he got 25 messages on Saturday.

So Mubin got 25 − 20 = **5 more** messages on Saturday than on Friday.

## Now Try These

1. Joanne gets a message when someone donates to her charity. The donations on Monday are shown below.

£9  £4  £7  £11  £5  £2  £6  £14  £13  £7  £15

a) Fill in the tally chart to show this information.

b) On Tuesday there were:
   • two fewer donations of £5 to £10
   • twice as many donations of more than £10

   Add this information to the pictogram below.

**Monday's Donations**

| Amount | Tally |
|---|---|
| Less than £5 | |
| £5 to £10 | |
| More than £10 | |

**Tuesday's Donations**   Key: ◯ = 2 donations

| | |
|---|---|
| Less than £5 | ◯ ◯ ◐ |
| £5 to £10 | |
| More than £10 | |

c) How many donations on Tuesday were £5 or more?

..............

d) How many more donations were there on Tuesday than on Monday?

..............

2. George wants to buy old phones at an auction.  He makes four bids:

| 1960s phone Bid: £100 | 1970s phone Bid: £150 | 1980s phone Bid: £125 | 1990s phone Bid: £75 |

a) Draw a bar chart to show this data.

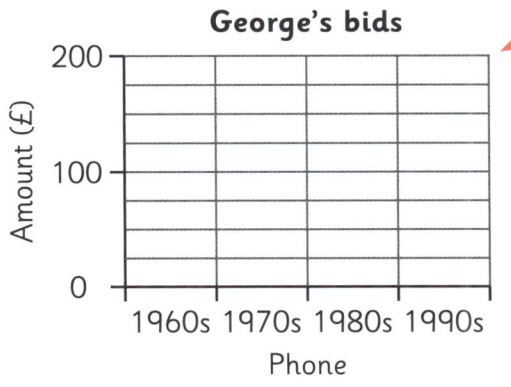 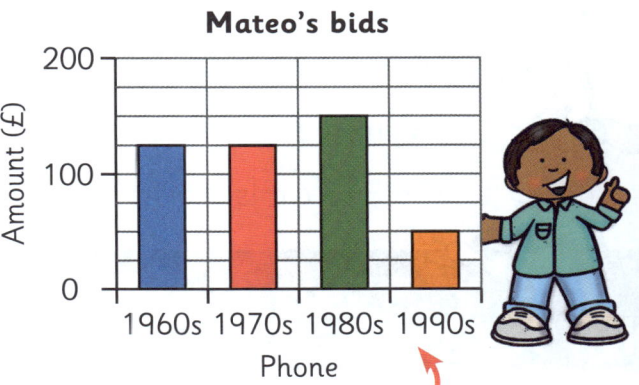

Mateo's bids for the same phones are shown in the bar chart above.

b) Use both bar charts to fill in this table to show the highest bid on each phone.

c) How much would George spend if he buys the phones that he has the higher bid for?

£ ....................

| Person | Phone | Bid (£) |
|---|---|---|
|  |  |  |
|  |  |  |
|  |  |  |
|  |  |  |

## An Extra Challenge

Alan and Fran draw a pictogram to show how many calls they made yesterday, but they've forgotten the key!  Work out how many calls they made in the afternoon.

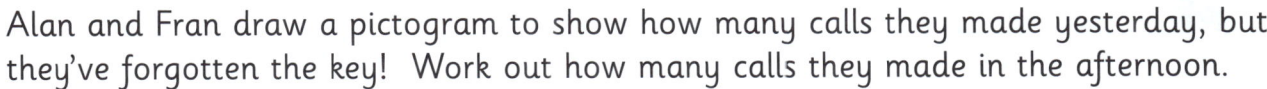

| Time of Day | Morning | Lunch | Afternoon |
|---|---|---|---|
| Number of Calls | 🕻🕻 | 🕻⌐ | ? |

We made two fewer calls at lunch than in the morning.

We made twice as many calls in the afternoon than in the morning.

Ring, ring... Hello?  It's me again — please tick a box!

  ☐  ☐  ☐

25

# Mixed Problems

Febe's Funhouse

## How It Works

You'll need to use more than one skill on trickier problems. Here's an example:

Make a length equal to $3\frac{1}{2}$ cm using **three** of these cards: [2] [mm] [3] [ml] [5]

First, convert 1 cm to 10 mm.

$3$ cm $= 3 \times 10 = 30$ mm and $\frac{1}{2}$ cm $= 10 \div 2 = 5$ mm

So $3\frac{1}{2}$ cm is the same as 35 mm. ⟶ [3] [5] [mm]

## Now Try These

1. How many right angles does the minute hand on a clock turn through when it moves from:

   a) 12 to 6?

   b) 7 to 4?

2. Drinks cost 60p each. Penny buys two drinks using one of the vouchers below. She pays 80p in total. Colour in the scissors under the voucher that she used.

   VOUCHER — Buy 2 drinks and get $\frac{1}{2}$ off.
   VOUCHER — Buy 2 drinks and get $\frac{1}{3}$ off.
   VOUCHER — Buy 2 drinks and get $\frac{1}{4}$ off.

3. A gumball machine has 50 balls of gum.
   The pictogram shows how many balls are sold each day.

   | Mon | Tue | Wed | Thu | Fri |
   |---|---|---|---|---|
   | 🔴◗ | 🔴🔴 | 🔴 | 🔴🔴 | 🔴 |

   Key: 🔴 = 4 balls

   The machine is not refilled.
   How many balls are left in the machine? .............. balls

26

4. Use the numbers in the bubbles to fill in the boxes and make correct calculations. Each part has a clue to help you.

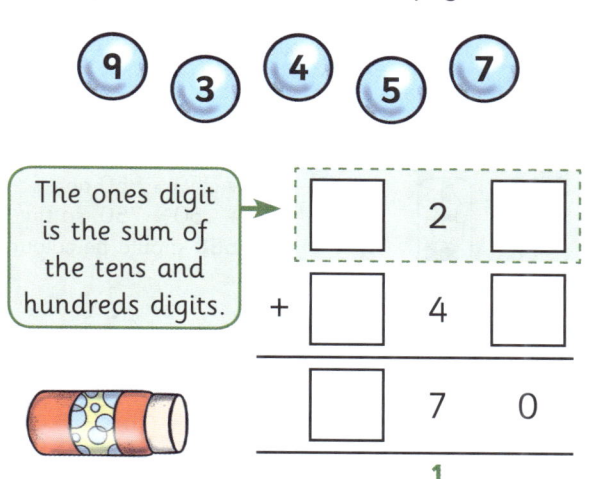

The ones digit is the sum of the tens and hundreds digits.

These digits are multiples of the same number (and it's not 1).

5. Look at the scales on the right. Each coloured block has the same shape and mass.

   a) What is the mass of one block? ............... g

   b) Circle the model with a total mass of 24 g.

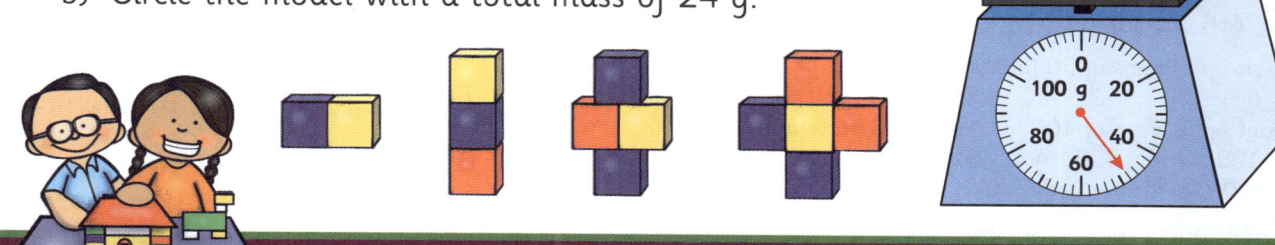

## An Extra Challenge

Febe's Funhouse sells these **toys** and **sweets**.

It also sells **lucky dip bags**. They cost **£5 each** and contain **1 toy** and **1 sweet**. Any of the items shown above could be inside.

a) How many different lucky dip bags are there?

b) What fraction of the bags are **cheaper** than buying the items they contain separately?

Sweet! How did these problems go for you?

27

# Answers

## Pages 2-3 — Working with Numbers 1

1.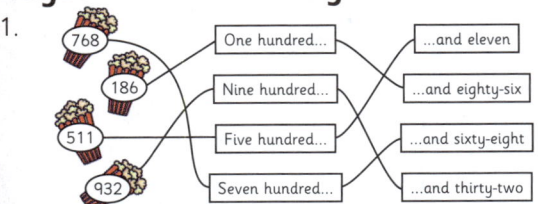
   768 — One hundred... ...and eighty-six
   186 — Nine hundred... ...and eleven
   511 — Five hundred... ...and sixty-eight
   932 — Seven hundred... ...and thirty-two

2. a) 632        b) 326

3. The number of people who saw Jigsaw Attack is 784. This is smaller than 814 and 786, so the posters for Vol-Tor-no and Deer Deer should be circled.

4. Beth's number is 437, so Matt's is 632.
   So Asha spent 392 minutes at the cinema.

   **An Extra Challenge**

   Each big drink shows 100, each medium drink shows 10 and each small drink shows 1.
   a) There is 1 large drink, 4 medium drinks and 5 small drinks, so the drinks show 145.
   b) There are now 6 large drinks, 4 medium drinks and 0 small drinks, so 640 is shown.

## Pages 4-5 — Working with Numbers 2

1. Count up in steps of 50 for the first pattern:
   0  50  100  150  200  250  **300**  350
   Count up in steps of 100 for the second pattern:
   0  100  200  **300**  400  500  600  700
   So **300** is hidden in both patterns.

2. a) The arrow is pointing about one quarter of the way between 180 and 220, so the number is about **190**.
   b) The arrow is pointing about halfway between 475 and 495, so the number is about **485**.

3. Brooke: 0, 4, **8**, 12, 16, **20**, 24, 28, 32, 36, ...
   Nora: 0, 8, 16, **24**, 32, 40, ...
   So **Brooke** says 5 − 3 = **2** more of the numbers.

4. There are 627 − 100 = 527 sticks left after the storm.
   So there are 527 + 10 + 10 + 10 = **557** sticks now.

   **An Extra Challenge**

   The arrow is pointing about halfway between 490 and 540, so the number is about 515.
   The tens digit is 1, so adding 3 gives 1 + 3 = 4.
   Now count on 5 lots of 4: 4 → 8 → 12 → 16 → 20 → 24.
   So there are **24 twigs** in the bundle.

## Pages 6-7 — Adding and Subtracting

1. 210 − 120 = 90, so the apple core is hiding **90**.
   675 − 475 = 200, so the cabbage leaf is hiding **200**.
   530 + 340 = 870, so the banana skin is hiding **870**.

2.  318      So they collected    ⁴5̶⁵9
   +241      559 bottles over    −472
   ‾559‾     the two days.        ‾ 87‾
   So they collected **87** more bottles than boxes.

3. a) [bottle: 850]
   b) 400 + 250 = 650 and 600 + 150 = 750, so the bin with **550** should be coloured in.

4.   683        945        1 ¹8
    + 56       −301       +784
    ‾739‾      ‾644‾      ‾902‾
      ¹                    ¹ ¹

   **An Extra Challenge**

   326 + 152 = 478 — the paper goes in the first bin.
   728 − 285 = 443 — the tin goes in the third bin.
   214 − 138 = 76 — the water bottle goes in the first bin.
   933 − 71 = 862 — the drink can goes in the
                    first or the second bin.
   309 + 131 = 440 — the glass bottle goes
                    in the first or the third bin.
   So the **drink can** and **glass bottle** are allowed in more than one of the bins.

## Pages 8-9 — Multiplying and Dividing

1. 4 × 10 × **2** = 80        2 × **10** × 3 = 60

2. 180 ÷ 3 = 60
   13 × 5 = 65 (10 × 5 = 50, 3 × 5 = 15, 50 + 15 = 65)
   33 × 2 = 66 (30 × 2 = 60, 3 × 2 = 6, 60 + 6 = 66)
   4 × 16 = 64 (10 × 4 = 40, 6 × 4 = 24, 40 + 24 = 64)
   64 is closest to 60, so the **4 × 16** T-shirt is his favourite.

3. The total number of swimmers is in the 3 times table, so the numbers that aren't in the 3 times table should be circled — **16** and **17**.

4. 40 × 8 = 320, 3 × 8 = 24, so
   43 × 8 = 320 + 24 = **344 strokes**.

5. a) 3 lemons are needed for 2 cups. 4 cups is twice as much, so 4 cups need 3 × 2 = **6 lemons**.
   b) (i) 2 cups need 400 ml, so
          1 cup needs 400 ÷ 2 = **200 ml**.
      (ii) 3 cups need 200 × 3 = **600 ml**.

6. 4 × 3 = **12 ways**

   **An Extra Challenge**

   Amaya has 4 × 6 = 24 lemons and 3 × 6 = 18 oranges. The oranges make 18 ÷ 2 = 9 lots of the recipe, but the lemons only make 24 ÷ 3 = 8 lots. The recipe is for 2 cups, so she can make at most 2 × 8 = **16 cups**.

## Pages 10-11 — Fractions

1. a) $\frac{2}{3} = \frac{4}{6}$, so 4 nuggets should be coloured in total.
   b) $\frac{2}{3} = \frac{4}{6}$ is smaller than $\frac{5}{6}$,
      and $\frac{1}{3}$ is smaller than $\frac{2}{3}$.
      So from largest to smallest: Josh, Eli, Kate.

28

# Answers

2. a) 3 out of 5 = $\frac{3}{5}$
   b) Find $\frac{3}{5}$ of 20: 20 ÷ 5 = 4, 4 × 3 = **12 beetles**

3. $\frac{4}{7} + \frac{2}{7} = \frac{6}{7}$    $\frac{8}{8} - \frac{3}{8} = \frac{5}{8}$
   E.g. $\frac{3}{6} + \frac{1}{6} = \frac{4}{6}$    E.g. $\frac{9}{10} - \frac{2}{10} = \frac{7}{10}$

4. a) Half an hour is 2 lots of 15 minutes, so he needs $\frac{4}{10} + \frac{4}{10} = \frac{8}{10}$ **kg** (or $\frac{4}{5}$ kg).
   b) Count on twice more in steps of $\frac{4}{10}$:
   $\frac{8}{10} + \frac{4}{10} = 1\frac{2}{10}$, $1\frac{2}{10} + \frac{4}{10} = 1\frac{6}{10}$ **kg** (or $1\frac{3}{5}$ kg)

### An Extra Challenge
a) $\frac{3}{10}$ = 6 rocks, so $\frac{1}{10}$ = 6 ÷ 3 = 2 rocks and $\frac{10}{10}$ = 2 × 10 = **20 rocks**.
b) $\frac{5}{10}$ of 20 = 5 × 2 = **10** pieces of quartz
   $\frac{2}{10}$ of 20 = 2 × 2 = **4** pieces of sandstone

## Pages 12-13 — Measuring

1. 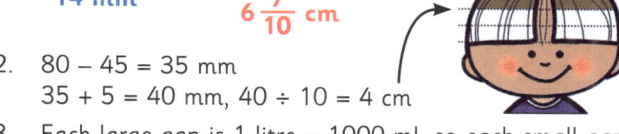 14 mm    6 $\frac{7}{10}$ cm

2. 80 − 45 = 35 mm
   35 + 5 = 40 mm, 40 ÷ 10 = 4 cm

3. Each large gap is 1 litre = 1000 ml, so each small gap is 500 ml. So the jugs contain 2500 ml + 3000 ml = **5500 ml** of water in total.

4.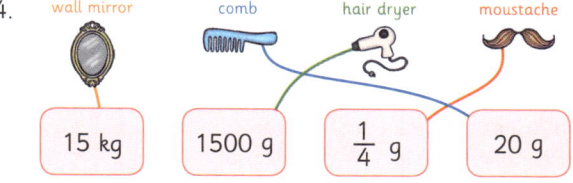

5. a) 2 hairbrushes have a mass of 240 g, so 1 hairbrush has a mass of 240 ÷ 2 = **120 g**.
   b) A hairbrush and a pair of scissors have a total mass of 170 g, so the scissors have a mass of 170 − 120 = **50 g**.

### An Extra Challenge
The 1st wig has a plait that's 22 cm long, which is a correct length. The 2nd wig has a plait that's 20 cm long, so it's too short. The 3rd wig has a plait that's 24 cm long, so it's too long. So **1 wig** is correct.

## Pages 14-15 — Mascot Muddle

- 483 + 179 = 662, so one vote goes to Seb Sun. The missing number is 530 − 340 = 190 and 595 − 405 = 190, so one vote goes to Tia Tiger.
- There are 7 × 4 = 28 different ways, so one vote goes to Wes Wolf. The missing number is 12 × 4 = 48, so one vote goes to Seb Sun.
- £5 = 500p and £3.70 = 370p, so the change is 500p − 370p = 130p and Tia Tiger gets a vote. The biggest amount with 2 coins is £1 + 20p = £1.20, so Fred Fox gets a vote.
- The shape with 1 pair of parallel sides and 1 pair of perpendicular sides is Wes Wolf's. His shape also has 1 right angle and 5 sides, so Wes Wolf gets both votes.
- At the end, Fred Fox has 1 vote, Sadie Storm has 0, Wes Wolf has 3, Seb Sun has 2 and Tia Tiger has 2. So the new mascot is **Wes Wolf**.

## Pages 16-17 — Money

1. £2 = 200p.  150p + 45p = 195p.
   £3 − 50p = 300p − 50p = 250p.
   £1.50 + 60p = 150p + 60p = 210p.
   £10 − £9.50 = 1000p − 950p = 50p.  So the boxes below **150p + 45p** and **£10 − £9.50** should be ticked.

2. She needs to save £300 − £90 = **£210** more.

3. The one he bought costs £50 − £15 = £35, so the chairs that cost more than £35 should be circled:

4. A £2 coin, a 50p coin and a 10p coin is £2.60, so **£2.60** should be circled.

5. a) A Sunshine Soup is 390p − 95p = 300p − 5p = 295p = **£2.95** cheaper.
   b) They cost 285p + 175p = 300p + 160p = 460p in total. You'll get 500p − 460p = 40p = **£0.40** as change.

### An Extra Challenge
Her purse has £10 − £4.80 = 1000p − 480p = 520p in coins. The first purse has £4 + 100p + 10p = 510p. The second purse has £4 + 50p + 30p = 480p. The last purse has £4 + 50p + 60p + 10p = 520p, so the **last purse** belongs to Nylah.

## Pages 18-19 — Time

1. March and April have 61 − 30 = 31 more days than June. March has 61 − 31 = 30 fewer days than November and December.

2. Iain takes 2 mins 10 seconds = 130 seconds. So the difference is 145 − 130 = **15 seconds**.

3. 3:10 pm →(+ 2 hours) 5:10 pm →(+ 30 mins) **5:40 pm**

4. a) The bus to Canary Wharf leaves at 10:55 and arrives at 11:50. This is 5 minutes less than an hour, so the journey takes **55 minutes**.
   b) The journey to Liverpool Street takes 40 minutes and the journey to Heathrow takes 50 minutes, so it is 50 − 40 = **10 minutes** quicker to travel to Liverpool Street.

# Answers

5. The clock shows about 1:51 = 13:51. Thirty minutes after this is 14:21. This is **9** minutes before 14:30, so he will be about **9** minutes early.

   **An Extra Challenge**

   a) 12:15 pm —60 mins→ 11:15 am —10 mins→ 11:05 am
   So Tim replaced the last guard at 11:05 am:
   
   b) The next guard will replace Tim 2 hours after 11:05 am, which is 1:05 pm:

   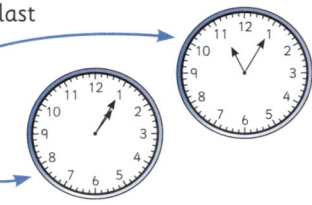

## Pages 20-21 — Shapes

1. There are lots of choices for the second shape. It must have 5 sides and they can't all be the same length. E.g.

2. a) faces   b) cylinder
   c) eight   d) vertices

3. Triangle: 3 cm + 4 cm + 5 cm = **12 cm**
   Trapezium: 4 cm + 2 cm + 2 cm + 2 cm = **10 cm**
   Pentagon: 4 cm + 1 cm + 3 cm + 3 cm + 1 cm = **12 cm**
   So the **trapezium** should be ticked.

4. You can see all of the cubes that make up each shape.
   a) **10** cubes   b) **6** cubes

5. Her shape is a pentagonal prism:
   It has **10** vertices, **15** edges and **7** faces.

   **An Extra Challenge**

   There are lots of different designs that could work. Each design needs three rectangles: one with a perimeter of **18 grid square sides**, one with a perimeter of **12 grid square sides** and one with a perimeter of **5 grid square sides**. E.g.

## Pages 22-23 — Angles and Lines

1. a) 2   b) 3
2. a)   b)
3. 
4. A: **2**   B: **0**   C: **5**
5. a)   b)

**An Extra Challenge**

a) and b) Here are some of the ways you can do it:

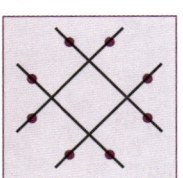 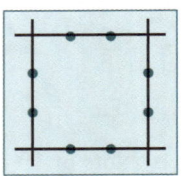 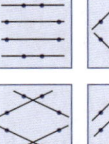 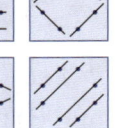

Your answer might look like one of these if you turn it.

## Pages 24-25 — Charts and Tables

1. a) 
   | Amount | Tally |
   |---|---|
   | Less than £5 | II |
   | £5 to £10 | IIII I |
   | More than £10 | IIII |

   b) 
   | Tuesday's Donations | Key:  = 2 donations |
   |---|---|
   | Less than £5 | ● ● ◐ |
   | £5 to £10 | ● ◐ |
   | More than £10 | ● ● ● |

   c) 3 + 8 = **11**   d) 16 – 11 = **5**

2. a) George's bids bar chart (1960s: 100, 1970s: 150, 1980s: 125, 1990s: 75)

   b) 
   | Person | Phone | Bid (£) |
   |---|---|---|
   | Mateo | 1960s | £125 |
   | George | 1970s | £150 |
   | Mateo | 1980s | £150 |
   | George | 1990s | £75 |

   c) £150 + £75 = **£225**

   **An Extra Challenge**

   The difference between Morning and Lunch is , so ☎ = 2 and ◠ = 4. They made ◠◠ = 4 + 4 = 8 calls in the morning. They made twice as many in the afternoon, so 2 × 8 = **16 calls**.

## Pages 26-27 — Mixed Problems

1. a) **2** right angles   b) **3** right angles

2. Two drinks normally cost 60p × 2 = 120p, so Penny got 120p – 80p = 40p off. $\frac{1}{3}$ of 120p = 120 ÷ 3 = 40p, so the scissors under the voucher with $\frac{1}{3}$ **off** should be coloured in.

3. 5 + 6 + 4 + 7 + 4 = 26 balls were sold in total.
   So 50 – 26 = **24 balls** are left in the machine.

4. ```
     5 2 7        ⁷¹³
   + 4 4 3      8 ̷8 ̷9
   ─────        - 4 5 3
     9 7 0      ───────
       ¹          3 8 6
   ```

5. a) 8 blocks have a mass of 48 g.
   So 1 block has a mass of 48 ÷ 8 = **6 g**.
   b) 4 × 6 = 24, so 4 blocks have a mass of 24 g. So this model should be circled:

   **An Extra Challenge**

   a) There are 2 × 3 = **6** different lucky dip bags.
   b) Only 2 bags have items that would cost more than £5 separately (the cube with the toffee apple or the chocolate), so the answer is $\frac{2}{6}$ (or $\frac{1}{3}$).
   ```